SandCastle™

Science Made Simple

It's Not Strange, I Know about Change!

Bridget Pederson

Consulting Editors, Diane Craig, M.A./Reading Specialist
and Susan Kosel, M.A. Education

Published by ABDO Publishing Company, 4940 Viking Drive, Edina, Minnesota 55435.

Printed in the United States.

Credits
Edited by: Pam Price
Curriculum Coordinator: Nancy Tuminelly
Cover and Interior Design and Production: Mighty Media
Photo Credits: AbleStock, Photodisc, ShutterStock, Wewerka Photography

Library of Congress Cataloging-in-Publication Data

Pederson, Bridget.
    It's not strange, I know about change! / Bridget Pederson.
      p. cm. -- (Science made simple)
    ISBN 10 1-59928-604-1 (hardcover)
    ISBN 10 1-59928-605-X (paperback)

    ISBN 13 978-1-59928-604-4 (hardcover)
    ISBN 13 978-1-59928-605-1 (paperback)
    1. Science--Methodology--Juvenile literature. 2. Observation (Scientific method)--Juvenile literature.
  I. Title.

  Q175.2.P43 2006
  500--dc22
                                                          2006023136

SandCastle Level: Transitional

SandCastle™ books are created by a professional team of educators, reading specialists, and content developers around five essential components—phonemic awareness, phonics, vocabulary, text comprehension, and fluency—to assist young readers as they develop reading skills and strategies and increase their general knowledge. All books are written, reviewed, and leveled for guided reading, early reading intervention, and Accelerated Reader® programs for use in shared, guided, and independent reading and writing activities to support a balanced approach to literacy instruction. The SandCastle™ series has four levels that correspond to early literacy development. The levels help teachers and parents select appropriate books for young readers.

Emerging Readers
(no flags)

Beginning Readers
(1 flag)

Transitional Readers
(2 flags)

Fluent Readers
(3 flags)

These levels are meant only as a guide. All levels are subject to change.

Change happens all around us every day! The earth, animals, plants, and people are always changing.

Words used to talk about change:
grow
living things
seasons
weather

The 🌍 is always changing.

When seen from , the appears to change shape.

An seed can grow and change into an apple .

Seasons change as the earth orbits the ☀.

All living things need food, , and air to change.

Habitats change if there is too much or too little 💧.

It's Not Strange, I Know about Change!

Jan plants some flower seeds.

She carefully waters.

She pulls any weeds.

When you plant a seed, you must be sure to give it what it needs.

12

Slowly the plant
begins to grow,
and each little leaf
starts to show.

Each leaf
of a plant
gets the sun
that its
roots can't.

13

Jan does not think
it is strange
when the plants
begin to change.
The flowers bloom
yellow and red,
and she picks some
for her friend Ted.

You can grow
flowers from seeds
when you give them
what they need.

15

Change Every Day!

Vance's flowers need sun, water, nutrients, and air to grow.

Plants are living things, just like people. All living things need food, water, and air.

18

Zoe doesn't like the rain. She hopes the weather will change tomorrow.

Weather changes all the time.

19

Barbara's puppy is growing. When he grows up, he will look like his parents.

Animals grow and change, just like people do!

21

22

As Ramon grows and changes, he loses his baby teeth and gets permanent teeth.

How have you changed as you have grown?

23

Glossary

habitat – the area or environment where a person or thing usually lives.

nutrient – something that helps living things grow. Vitamins, minerals, and proteins are nutrients.

orbit – to move in a circular path around something.

permanent – meant to last for a very long time.